ARTIST ARCHIVES™ INTRODUCTION BY MAX ALLAN COLLINS

ELVGREN GIRLS II

COLLECTORS PRESS®

PORTLAND, OREGON

COPYRIGHT © 1999 COLLECTORS PRESS, INC.

Design   Principia Graphica
Technical Assistance   Hoover H.Y. Li
Editor   Ann Granning Bennett

The publisher would like to extend a special thanks to Ron Buol for
supplying various images in this book.

Printed in China

Library of Congress Cataloging-in-Publication Data
Collins, Max Allan.
        Elvgren girls II / Max Allan Collins. — 1st American ed.
            p. cm. — (Artist archives)
        Companion vol. to Elvgren girls I.
        ISBN 1-888054-34-4 (pbk. : alk. paper)
        1. Elvgren, Gillette. 2. Women in art 3. Pinup art — United
    States. I. Title. II. Title: Elvgren girls 2. III. Title:
    Elvgren girls two. IV. Series.
    ND237.E585A4 1999a
    759.13 — dc21   99-29640
                                                         CIP

98765432

FOR A FREE CATALOG WRITE TO COLLECTORS PRESS, INC.

P.O. Box 230986
Portland, Oregon 97281
Toll Free 800-423-1848
Or visit our website at *www.collectorspress.com*

ELVGREN
—
GIRLS II

INTRODUCTION

THE PIN-UPS in this book are the early, seminal work of an artist whose images were a familiar part of the American landscape from World War Two until the early 1970s. While Gil Elvgren's name itself was known in advertising circles as an imprimatur of quality, where "pretty girl" illustration was concerned, the artist did not achieve the household-name recognition of George Petty or Alberto Vargas, despite the widespread even pervasive presence of his work all across America.

Primarily in an exquisite series of calendar paintings for the Brown & Bigelow Company of St. Paul, Minnesota, Elvgren's glowing, wholesome girls-next-door became friendly icons of Americana, as much a symbol of the 1940s, 1950s, and 1960s sensuality as Betty Grable, Marilyn Monroe, or Raquel Welch. Elvgren girls seemed to say that sex and romance were inextricably linked and there was nothing dirty about it — one of the healthiest messages advertising sent in those often repressed years.

Today, through books like this one, a name has finally been attached to these sexy slices of nostalgia: Gil Elvgren has at long last joined the roster of pin-up greats that includes Vargas and Petty, eclipsing giants of their day such as Rolf Armstrong, Earl Moran, and Earl MacPherson. Why has it taken so long for Elvgren to achieve recognition?

It's not surprising, really. After all, Elvgren's lush brushstroke style was an extension of that of his mentor, Haddon Sundblom, whose Coca-Cola ads (particularly his Santas) were already icons of American advertising; and Elvgren's own soft-drink sweethearts are virtually indistinguishable from his teacher's. Other students of Sundblom followed Elvgren's lead into creating pin-ups in oil on canvas, working in the same painterly style.

The casual eye of fraternal lodge brothers or barbershop and auto-garage patrons could hardly be expected to tell Elvgren from such talented peers as (among others) Art Frahm, Edward D'Acona, Edward Runci, Al Buell, and Bill Medcalf, much less Elvgren's own assistants, Joyce Ballantyne and Harry Ekman. The men who enjoyed Elvgren's pin-ups — and those of his peers — simply knew a pretty girl in a cute, compromising situation when they saw it. And enjoyed it.

Still, Elvgren stands apart from these other artists, in part because his craft was superior in a field crowded with terrific illustrators; but more so because he was an innovator. Yes, Elvgren paid lip service to the cliches and conventions of an already reviled, low-brow form, chiefly those established by George Petty (and his Esquire successor, Alberto Vargas), whose lovely subjects tended to float in a nonspecific background with perhaps a single prop, often a phone with Petty or an oversize hat with Vargas.

A number of the images in this book reveal Elvgren sticking to that pattern (imitating Petty, not Vargas, who was not yet a significant presence) and isolating his subjects, sending girls adrift in a sea of solid color, often blue or yellow or maybe a mauve-ish pink. Petty's favorite prop, the telephone and its wire, is often replaced in Elvgren by the leash of a naughty dog, the line of the leash serving much the same design purpose as Petty's phone cord. "Blind Date," the striking image that graces our cover,

or the similarly fetching "Help Wanted" and "Skirting Trouble" demonstrate use of this element.

But in "Blind Date," despite certain deco abstractions out of Petty, our startled brunette inhabits at least a suggestion of a realistic setting; despite the cartoonish outline of the table, the coffee pot and china are substantial and real, the window blinds walking a line between their use as a design element and representational illustration. The presence of an animal is typical in Elvgren: that the artist chose living creatures as his favorite "prop" is telling. George Petty rarely included animals, and his settings tended toward vague cartoonish streaks of crayon.

Petty depicting phones and stools and other props with a simple line drawing (usually red) evolved from the artist's initial tenure at Esquire as a panel cartoonist. Further, Petty intended to send what today would be considered an incredibly sexist message: that a pretty girl is the key "object" in his pared-down world.

Working from photos of models he had taken and posed himself, Elvgren always viewed his subjects as more real than that — hence the world around his beauties included other living creatures and carefully selected, realistically depicted elements of that world. The lushly rendered "Weight Control" has a typical flat background (though its gray tone is somewhat atypical, as Elvgren preferred bright colors against which to position his pin-up girls). But it also contains a rug, a pillow, and the weight machine the girl is utilizing.

The abstraction of the bright blue background of "A Pleasing Discovery" — with its rare, if innocent, use of nudity — is offset by the presence of a cute cocker spaniel and the reality of the scale the girl is perched upon. "Catch On" merges another abstract blue background with the blue of water and features a very illustrational-style dock, a fishing basket, and three living creatures: a Scottish terrier, a scavenging bird, and a lovely fishergal (and a deceased fish).

Such subjects separate Elvgren from the cartoon school of Petty. Elvgren was a traditional illustrator who brought to the female form a painterly style and a full palette of oils on canvas, following the footsteps of Haddon Sundblom and John Singer Sargent, and not George Petty and Rolf Armstrong.

In fact, Gil Elvgren rejected most of what the most contemporary popular pin-up artists were up to and in so doing forged his place as an innovator in the genre. Petty was a master of watercolor and airbrush; Armstrong was a virtuoso of pastels, as was future Marilyn Monroe discoverer, Earl Moran. A young artist in 1937 might have been expected to follow these established, popular pin-up pros, and to a limited extent Elvgren did — Moran's subject matter and use of a more extended library of props obviously had more impact than Petty or Armstrong on Elvgren.

Even so, Moran worked in pastels and Elvgren worked in oils, and, largely by choosing this medium, Elvgren created a new pin-up style. This was a matter of experimentation, of trial and error, and these early pin-ups — his first, a group done for the Louis Dow Company in the late 1930s and early 1940s — show him working toward the balanced approach of his later Brown & Bigelow masterpieces. Elvgren's painterly technique made the simplistic pin-up image on a field of solid color seem wanting, somehow, and even in his earliest paintings Elvgren can be seen suggesting a real, complete world for his sexy subjects to occupy. A girl-next-door, after all, requires a door.

And even in his most simplistic images — which seem at first glance to contain nothing but the girl — objects and background items make themselves known. My favorite pin-up in this book, "Thar She Blows!" (did this inspire the famous scene in "Seven Year Itch"?) has a solid red background for our green-dressed proto-Marilyn Monroe to stand against, but the wind blowing up her skirt comes from a very specific looking nozzle, and the letters of the funhouse sign — though floating themselves — have solid reality. In "The High Sign," the lovely blonde hitchhiker sits upon a very real suitcase beside an equally sturdy road sign; and another blonde hitchhiker places her on foot on her bag in "Foot Loose," as she seeks a ride, Claudette Colbert / "It Happened One Night" style.

"Caught in the Draft" again uses mostly an abstract blue background, but the blonde caught in the rain has a transparent though tangible umbrella, as she dances through a suggestion of raindrops and puddles via some impressionistic dollops of white. Another blonde caught in the rain, in "Disturbing Elements," has a darker impression of sky as a background and streaks of white rain — but a most solid trunk as she snuggles beneath an umbrella . . . though why, exactly, she is hiking her skirt remains a mystery (only few Elvgren fans will mind).

One of the artist's finest early pin-ups — "Station WOW" — is replete with deco-ish elements and Petty-esque touches, particularly the cartoonish floating music notes. Yet despite the almost overwhelming yellow backdrop into which it fades, the *art moderne* radio is a most solid prop, as is the pad the dark-haired beauty rests upon as she kicks at the air in time to the music.

Another one of these early images suggest the more complete backgrounds common in later Elvgren works: the bewitching redhead climbing into an upper berth inhabits a train setting that seems real indeed, though much of it disappears into darkness while the glowing pillow and covers paint their own enticing picture. "A Lad-Her Problem," depicting an elopement (not bothering us with the groom-to-be), is complete enough to be a magazine illustration.

Like Norman Rockwell, with whom he has so often been compared, Elvgren is at heart an illustrator, and an illustrator needs a story to tell. His best pin-ups tell little tales often tied to everyday American life, paintings depicting All-American girls who, in the musings of GIs dreaming of the postwar world, might well live next door.

In these pages, Elvgren tells the story of embarrassed young women whose dresses are snagged by leashes and whipped by wind, poor victim-

ized lasses whose direct gazes drip with such coy chagrin that the suspicion arises they have somehow orchestrated or at least allowed these enticing "embarrassments" to occur.

Elvgren will tell you tales of hitchhiking honeys hiking their skirts for a ride; of healthy young women refining their figures through exercise, and showing off those works in progress via scanty workout togs suspiciously resembling lingerie. The artist will sing songs of silk stockings and garter belts. He will spin yarns of cuties caught in the act of readying themselves for bed or checking their weight in the nude or simply fishing off a pier in a two-piece sunsuit no more unlikely than the beauty of its wearer.

Through these stories of sweet sexuality, Elvgren helped create the ideal of feminine beauty in the second half of the twentieth century — the girls GIs rushed home to marry. It's only fair that he also defined and recorded the postwar era in all its commercial glory for clients including Coca-Cola, General Electric, NAPA auto parts, beer companies, and even Ovaltine — for the kids those beautiful wives produced.

Gil Elvgren continued painting calendar girls and creating pretty-girl advertising art into the early 1970s, long past the demand for such work. But finally the market dried up almost entirely, leaving him frustrated and somewhat bewildered. America finally had passed him by.

The artist's death in 1980 was noted by only a relative handful of pin-up buffs; his last pretty-girl calendar appeared posthumously, in 1981. But in the intervening years, the interest in pin-ups, and Elvgren's work in particular, has grown steadily.

The images in this book represent Elvgren at the start of his career, the period in which he was creating and defining what would be an enduring American icon; the pretty girl-next-door.

In sheer stockings.

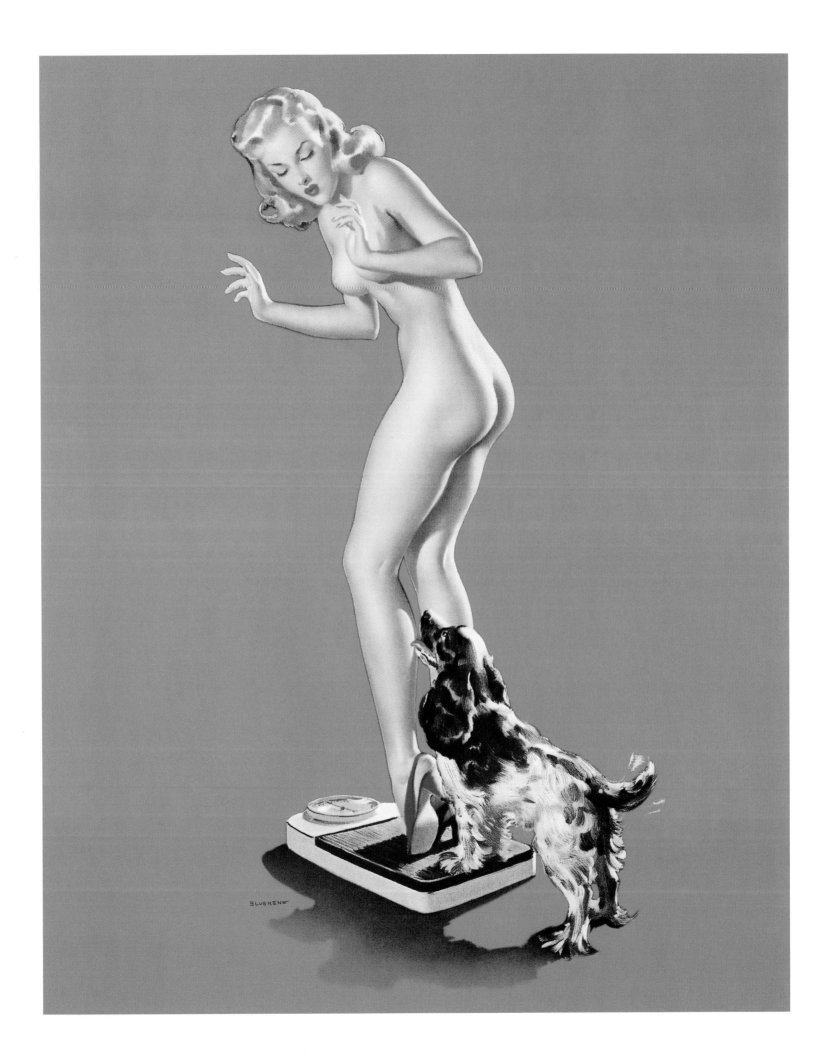